foreword

Bake, boil, fry, foil; pipe, mash, stuff, hash—is there anything you can't do with a potato? Because it's so versatile, it's an easy answer when you're wondering about what to serve along with your entree. And because this root vegetable is so healthy—a medium spud is fat-free and has 100 calories and 45 per cent of your daily vitamin C requirements—it's a guilt-free side solution too!

To help you explore the delights of this delicious vegetable, Company's Coming has pulled together some of its best recipes for this convenient little book. Whether it's crisp wedges, toothsome gnocchi or creamy mashed potatoes, there are enough side-dish ideas to suit family meals as well as special gatherings. With spuds this splendid, they're sure to become the stars of your table.

Jean Paré

herbed potatoes

New or baby potatoes, with flimsy, parchment-like skin, are those harvested in the spring or early summer. They're prized for their high moisture content and creamy texture.

Baby potatoes, larger ones cut in half	1 1/2 lbs.	680 g
Cooking oil	2 tsp.	10 mL
Dried oregano	1 tsp.	5 mL
Ground savory	1 tsp.	5 mL
Parsley flakes	1 tsp.	5 mL
Seasoned salt	1/2 tsp.	2 mL

Put potatoes into large bowl. Drizzle with cooking oil. Toss until coated.

Sprinkle with remaining 4 ingredients. Toss until coated. Arrange in single layer on ungreased baking sheet. Bake in 350°F (175°C) oven for about 45 minutes until tender. Serves 4.

1 serving: 134 Calories; 2.5 g Total Fat (1.4 g Mono, 0.8 g Poly, 0.2 g Sat); 0 mg Cholesterol; 25 g Carbohydrate; 2 g Fibre; 3 g Protein; 159 mg Sodium

potatoes on a stick

The first potatoes of the season are memorable when prepared this way. Fresh sprigs of the herbs used in the recipe are always appropriate for garnish.

Red baby potatoes, larger ones cut in half	10	10
White baby potatoes, larger ones cut in half	10	10
Olive (or cooking) oil	2 tbsp.	30 mL
Dried basil	1/2 tsp.	2 mL
Dried oregano	1/2 tsp.	2 mL
Ground rosemary	1/8 tsp.	0.5 mL
Seasoned salt	1 tsp.	5 mL
Pepper, sprinkle		
Metal skewers (12 inches, 30 cm, each)	4	4

Pour water into large saucepan until about 1 inch (2.5 cm) deep. Add red and white potatoes. Cover. Bring to a boil. Reduce heat to medium. Boil gently for 5 minutes. Drain. Let stand for 10 minutes.

Combine next 6 ingredients in small bowl. Set aside.

Thread potatoes, alternating red and white, onto skewers. Brush with olive oil mixture. Preheat electric grill for 5 minutes. Cook skewers on greased grill for about 30 minutes, turning occasionally and brushing with remaining olive oil mixture, until tender. Makes 4 skewers.

1 skewer: 191 Calories; 7.1 g Total Fat (1.2 g Mono, 0.6 g Poly, 0.1 g Sat); 4 mg Cholesterol; 30 g Carbohydrate; 3 g Fibre; 3 g Protein; 347 mg Sodium

hasselback potatoes

Oprah Winfrey claims that her idea of heaven is a great big baked potato and someone to share it with. This recipe updates the look of the classic. Use your favourite seasoning salt as a variation.

Medium smooth oval unpeeled baking potatoes	8	8
Butter (or hard margarine), softened	2 tbsp.	30 mL
Salt, sprinkle		
Pepper, sprinkle		

Make crosswise cuts in tops of potatoes, 1/4 inch (6 mm) apart, almost, but not quite through, to bottom. Arrange, cut-side up, in greased 9 x 13 inch (22 x 33 cm) baking dish. Pat tops dry with paper towel.

Spread potatoes with half of butter. Sprinkle with salt and pepper. Bake, uncovered, in 450°F (230°C) oven for about 40 minutes, spreading with remaining butter at halftime. Serves 8.

1 serving: 125 Calories; 2.8 g Total Fat (0.7 g Mono, 0.1 g Poly, 1.8 g Sat); 8 mg Cholesterol; 26 g Carbohydrate; 3 g Fibre; 4 g Protein; 20 mg Sodium

bacon and cheese spuds

These rich-tasting, lower-fat potatoes can be a meal in themselves served alongside a salad. Extra toppings such as salsa or tomato slices boost the vegetable nutrients.

Medium unpeeled potatoes	4	4
Grated light sharp Cheddar cheese	1/4 cup	60 mL
Herb-flavoured non-fat cream cheese	1/4 cup	60 mL
Milk	1 tbsp.	15 mL
Salt	1/4 tsp.	1 mL
Pepper	1/16 tsp.	0.5 mL
Bacon slices, diced	3	3
Chopped fresh white mushrooms	1/2 cup	125 mL
Chopped green onion	2 tbsp.	30 mL
Grated light sharp Cheddar cheese	1/4 cup	60 mL

Poke several holes randomly with fork into potatoes. Bake in 375°F (190°C) oven for 1 1/4 hours until tender. Remove to wire rack. Let stand until cool enough to handle. Cut 1/4 inch (6 mm) piece lengthwise from top of potatoes. Scoop pulp into medium bowl, leaving 1/4 inch (6 mm) thick shells. Arrange on ungreased baking sheet. Set aside. Mash pulp.

Add next 5 ingredients. Beat until smooth.

Cook bacon in medium frying pan on medium for 3 to 4 minutes until crisp. Remove bacon with slotted spoon to cheese mixture, reserving 1 tbsp. (15 mL) bacon.

Drain all but 1 tsp. (5 mL) drippings. Add mushrooms and green onion. Cook, stirring often, until mushrooms are softened. Stir into cheese mixture. Spoon into potato shells.

Sprinkle with second amount of Cheddar cheese and reserved bacon. Bake in 350°F (175°C) oven for about 20 minutes until heated through. Makes 4 stuffed potatoes.

1 stuffed potato: 187 Calories; 5.4 g Total Fat (1.4 g Mono, 0.4 g Poly, 2.6 g Sat); 16 mg Cholesterol; 28 g Carbohydrate; 4 g Fibre; 12 g Protein; 445 mg Sodium

golden potato cups

The presentation of these stuffed, baked potatoes creates a contemporary look for an old favourite! No pastry bag? Just spoon the stuffing into the shells. You can assemble and refrigerate the potato cups up to a day ahead, and bake as directed for an extra 10 minutes.

Medium unpeeled baking potatoes	3	3
Large fresh unpeeled orange-fleshed sweet potato, halved	1	1
Cooking oil	1 tsp.	5 mL
Chopped fresh chives	1 tbsp.	15 mL
Salt	1/4 tsp.	1 mL
Pepper	1/8 tsp.	0.5 mL
Ground nutmeg, just a pinch		
Melted butter (or hard margarine)	2 tsp.	10 mL

Chopped fresh chives, for garnish

Poke several holes randomly with fork in potatoes and sweet potato halves. Brush potatoes and sweet potato halves with cooking oil. Place on ungreased baking sheet. Bake in 350°F (175°C) oven for about 1 1/2 hours until tender. Let stand for about 10 minutes until cool enough to handle. Scoop out pulp from sweet potato into large bowl. Cover to keep warm. Cut potatoes in half crosswise (inset photo). Trim thin slice from bottom of each half so it will sit flat. Scoop out pulp into same large bowl, leaving 1/4 inch (6 mm) thick shells.

Add next 4 ingredients. Mash until smooth. Spoon into pastry bag fitted with large star tip. Place potato shells on greased baking sheet. Pipe potato mixture into shells.

Brush with melted butter. Bake in 375°F (190°C) oven for about 20 minutes until heated through.

Garnish with second amount of chives. Makes 6 potato cups.

1 potato cup: 182 Calories; 2.4 g Total Fat (0.8 g Mono, 0.4 g Poly, 0.9 g Sat); 4 mg Cholesterol; 37 g Carbohydrate; 4 g Fibre; 4 g Protein; 130 mg Sodium

crispy spiced potatoes

This tasty, low-fat side pairs wonderfully with barbecued steak or pork chops. A salad can round out the meal.

Egg whites (large)	2	2
Large unpeeled red potatoes, cut into 8 wedges each	4	4
Chopped fresh rosemary	2 tsp.	10 mL
Lemon pepper	1 tsp.	5 mL
Garlic powder	1/2 tsp.	2 mL
Ground cumin	1/2 tsp.	2 mL

Beat egg whites in extra-large bowl until frothy. Do not overbeat. Add potato. Toss until coated. Arrange in single layer on greased baking sheet.

Combine remaining 4 ingredients in small cup. Sprinkle over potato. Bake in 400°F (205°C) oven for about 1 hour, turning at halftime, until golden and crisp. Makes 32 wedges.

4 wedges: 122 Calories; 0.2 g Total Fat (0 g Mono, 0.1 g Poly, 0 g Sat); 0 mg Cholesterol; 26 g Carbohydrate; 3 g Fibre; 4 g Protein; 25 mg Sodium

greek lemon potatoes

If you're really in a hurry, don't peel the potatoes. Most of their fibre is in the skin, and many of the nutrients are just underneath it. Wash them well and enjoy!

Medium peeled potatoes, quartered	8	8
Lemon juice	3 tbsp.	50 mL
Hard margarine (or butter), melted	2 tbsp.	30 mL
Olive (or cooking) oil	2 tbsp.	30 mL
Dried oregano	1 1/2 tsp.	7 mL
Salt	1 1/2 tsp.	7 mL
Pepper, sprinkle		
Hot water	2/3 cup	150 mL

Rinse potato. Put into extra-large bowl. Drizzle with next 3 ingredients. Toss until coated. Sprinkle with next 3 ingredients. Toss until coated.

Pour hot water into roasting pan. Add potato. Do not stir. Bake, uncovered, in 400°F (205°C) oven for 45 to 60 minutes, shaking pan and adding more hot water, if necessary, to prevent sticking, until tender and golden brown. Serves 8.

1 serving: 147 Calories; 6.5 g Total Fat (4.4 g Mono, 0.6 g Poly, 1.1 g Sat); 0 mg Cholesterol; 21 g Carbohydrate; 2 g Fibre; 2 g Protein; 486 mg Sodium

taco potato wedges with guacamole

If you love tacos and big wedge fries, these are the potatoes for you!
The easy-to-make guacamole is great with other Tex-Mex dishes too.

Large unpeeled potatoes, cut into 12 wedges each	2	2
Cooking oil	1 tbsp.	15 mL
Taco seasoning mix, stirred before measuring	2 tbsp.	30 mL
GUACAMOLE		
Ripe medium avocados	2	2
Sour cream	1/4 cup	60 mL
Green onions, chopped	2	2
Chili sauce	1 tbsp.	15 mL
Lemon juice	1 tbsp.	15 mL
Garlic clove, minced (or 1/4 tsp., 1 mL, powder)	1	1
Salt, sprinkle		

Put potato into large bowl. Drizzle with cooking oil. Toss until coated.
Sprinkle with seasoning. Toss until coated. Arrange in single layer on
ungreased baking sheet. Bake in 375°F (190°C) oven for about 45 minutes,
turning once, until golden. Makes 24 wedges.

Guacamole: Mash avocados in medium bowl until smooth. Add remaining
6 ingredients. Mix well. Makes about 1 1/2 cups (375 mL) guacamole.
Transfer to small serving bowl. Set on platter. Surround with potato
wedges. Serves 6.

*1 serving: 266 Calories; 14.3 g Total Fat (8.2 g Mono, 2.1 g Poly, 2.7 g Sat); 4 mg Cholesterol;
33 g Carbohydrate; 5 g Fibre; 5 g Protein; 390 mg Sodium*

easy crispy dippers

Potato versatility at its best. This kid-friendly side can do double-duty as a halftime or between-periods snack! Couch potatoes will adore these tasty wedges, perfect with our tangy mustard and bacon dip.

Large peeled potatoes, cut into 8 wedges each	6	6
Olive (or cooking) oil	2 tbsp.	30 mL
Dried rosemary, crushed	1 tbsp.	15 mL
Garlic salt	1 tsp.	5 mL
Coarsely ground pepper	1 tsp.	5 mL
MUSTARD AND BACON DIP		
Sour cream	1/2 cup	125 mL
Dijon mustard (with whole seeds)	2 tbsp.	30 mL
Bacon slices, cooked crisp and crumbled	3	3
Green onions, finely sliced	2	2

Put potato into large bowl. Drizzle with olive oil. Toss until coated. Add remaining 3 ingredients. Toss until coated. Arrange in single layer on greased baking sheet with sides. Bake in 400°F (205°C) oven for about 50 minutes, turning once, until browned.

Mustard and Bacon Dip: Combine all 4 ingredients in small bowl. Makes about 3/4 cup (175 mL) dip. Serve with potato wedges. Serves 8.

1 serving: 199 Calories; 7.2 g Total Fat (3.8 g Mono, 0.7 g Poly, 2.3 g Sat); 8 mg Cholesterol; 30 g Carbohydrate; 3 g Fibre; 5 g Protein; 258 mg Sodium

home fries

Leftover boiled potatoes make this an easy, tasty brunch dish. Omit the ham if vegetarians are on the guest list.

Cooking oil	1 tbsp.	15 mL
Chopped onion	1 cup	250 mL
Chopped green pepper	1/2 cup	125 mL
Chopped red pepper	1/2 cup	125 mL
Medium peeled potatoes, cooked and cubed	6	6
Chopped deli ham	1 cup	250 mL
Salt, sprinkle		
Pepper, sprinkle		

Heat cooking oil in large frying pan on medium. Add next 3 ingredients. Cook for 5 to 10 minutes, stirring often, until onion is golden and peppers are soft.

Add potato and ham. Sprinkle with salt and pepper. Cook for about 10 minutes, stirring often, until heated through. Serves 8.

1 serving: 181 Calories; 4.9 g Total Fat (1.3 g Mono, 0.9 g Poly, 1.3 g Sat); 16 mg Cholesterol; 28 g Carbohydrate; 3 g Fibre; 7 g Protein; 17 mg Sodium

fennel potatoes

In the Mediterranean, wild fennel flourishes by the roadside. When buying this licorice-scented vegetable, look for firm, white bulbs, with no brown or yellow spots, topped with fresh, green, feathery leaves.

Olive (or cooking) oil	2 tbsp.	30 mL
Thinly sliced fennel bulb (white part only)	2 cups	500 mL
Red baby potatoes, cut into 8 wedges each	1 lb.	454 g
Lemon pepper	1/2 tsp.	2 mL
Roasted red pepper, cut into strips	1 cup	250 mL
Prepared chicken broth	3 tbsp.	50 mL

Heat olive oil in large frying pan on medium-high. Add next 3 ingredients. Cook for about 5 minutes, stirring often, until potato and fennel start to brown. Reduce heat to medium.

Add red pepper and broth. Stir. Cook, covered, for about 10 minutes, stirring occasionally until potato is tender. Serves 4.

1 serving: 213 Calories; 7.4 g Total Fat (5.0 g Mono, 0.7 g Poly, 0.9 g Sat); 0 mg Cholesterol; 35 g Carbohydrate; 8 g Fibre; 5 g Protein; 261 mg Sodium

tapas potatoes brava

These spicy, Spanish-style potatoes are often served as a room-temperature appetizer, but we think you'll love them as an accompaniment to any barbecued dinner.

Olive (or cooking) oil	3 tbsp.	50 mL
Red baby potatoes, cut in half	1 lb.	454 g
All-purpose flour	1 tsp.	5 mL
Paprika	1 tsp.	5 mL
Brown sugar, packed	1/2 tsp.	2 mL
Cayenne pepper	1/4 – 1/2 tsp.	1 – 2 mL
Can of tomato sauce	7 1/2 oz.	213 mL
Green onions, sliced	2	2
Red wine vinegar	1 tbsp.	15 mL

Heat olive oil in large frying pan on medium-high. Add potatoes. Cook for about 2 minutes, stirring constantly, until browned.

Combine next 4 ingredients in small cup. Sprinkle over potatoes. Toss until coated.

Add remaining 3 ingredients. Bring to a boil. Reduce heat to medium-low. Simmer, covered, for about 15 minutes until potatoes are tender. Simmer, uncovered, for about 4 minutes until sauce is slightly thickened. Serve warm or at room temperature. Makes about 4 cups (1 L). Serves 4.

1 serving: 199 Calories; 10.6 g Total Fat (7.6 g Mono, 1.0 g Poly, 1.5 g Sat); 0 mg Cholesterol; 25 g Carbohydrate; 3 g Fibre; 3 g Protein; 342 mg Sodium

hot potato salad

Boil the potatoes whole and then peel them for this quick, easy-to-make recipe. And if you're short on time, don't bother peeling them.

Bacon slices, diced	6	6
Cubed cooked potato	4 cups	1 L
Green onions, sliced	4	4
Chopped celery	1/2 cup	125 mL
Italian dressing	1/2 cup	125 mL
Grated Parmesan cheese	1/2 cup	125 mL

Cook bacon in large frying pan on medium, stirring often, until crisp. Transfer with slotted spoon to paper towels. Set aside. Drain all but 1 tsp. (5 mL) drippings.

Add next 4 ingredients to same frying pan. Cook for about 8 minutes, stirring often, until heated through. Transfer to large bowl.

Add bacon and cheese. Stir. Serve immediately. Serves 4.

1 serving: 438 calories; 30.3 g Total Fat (15.3 g Mono, 7.9 g Poly, 5.7 g Sat); 39 mg Cholesterol; 32 g Carbohydrate; 3 g Fibre; 12 g Protein; 911 mg Sodium

spicy potato bumps

Here's a chance to take your spice rack for a test drive. Remember to keep your spices out of direct sunlight, heat and humidity to preserve their freshness.

Medium unpeeled baking potatoes, cubed	6	6
Olive (or cooking) oil	1 tbsp.	15 mL
Parsley flakes	2 tsp.	10 mL
Salt	1 1/2 tsp.	7 mL
Chili powder	1 tsp.	5 mL
Paprika	1 tsp.	5 mL
Dried thyme	1/2 tsp.	2 mL
Garlic powder	1/4 tsp.	1 mL
Cayenne pepper	1/8 tsp.	0.5 mL
Dried rosemary, crushed	1/8 tsp.	0.5 mL

Put potato into large bowl. Drizzle with olive oil. Toss until coated.

Combine remaining 8 ingredients in small cup. Sprinkle over potato. Toss until coated. Spread on large greased baking sheet with sides. Bake on centre rack in 425°F (220°C) oven for about 45 minutes, stirring twice, until tender and browned. Makes about 6 cups (1.5 L). Serves 6.

1 serving: 134 Calories; 2.6 g Total Fat (1.7 g Mono, 0.3 g Poly, 0.4 g Sat); 0 mg Cholesterol; 25 g Carbohydrate; 3 g Fibre; 3 g Protein; 694 mg Sodium

easy potato casserole

Assemble this casserole in the morning and have the kids pop it into the oven before you get home from work. To prepare the onion soup mix, place it in a resealable plastic bag and crush with a rolling pin.

Peeled potatoes, cut up	4 lbs.	1.8 kg
Hard margarine (or butter), melted	1/4 cup	60 mL
Envelope onion soup mix, crushed	1 1/2 oz.	42 g

Green onion pieces, for garnish
Sour cream, for garnish

Put potato into extra-large bowl. Drizzle with melted margarine. Toss until coated. Sprinkle with soup mix. Toss until coated. Transfer to greased 3 quart (3 L) casserole dish. Bake, covered, in 350°F (175°C) oven for about 1 1/4 hours until tender.

Garnish with green onion and sour cream. Makes about 11 cups (2.75 L).

1 cup (250 mL): 175 Calories; 4.9 g Total Fat (3.1 g Mono, 0.5 g Poly, 1.0 g Sat); trace Cholesterol; 30 g Carbohydrate; 3 g Fibre; 4 g Protein; 404 mg Sodium

spicy baked potatoes and onions

In the 1700s, Marie Antoinette gave her celebrity endorsement to a new South American vegetable by wearing potato blossoms in her hair. If she'd offered her subjects this dish instead, history might have been changed!

Large unpeeled baking potatoes, cut up	5	5
Medium onions, cut into 8 pieces each	2	2
Hard margarine (or butter), melted	2 tbsp.	30 mL
Dried basil	1 tsp.	5 mL
Seasoned salt	1 tsp.	5 mL
Cayenne pepper	1/8 tsp.	0.5 mL
Garlic powder	1/8 tsp.	0.5 mL

Sour cream, for garnish
Sprig of fresh basil, for garnish

Put potato and onion into large bowl. Combine next 5 ingredients in small cup. Drizzle over potato mixture. Toss until coated. Transfer to ungreased 9 x 13 inch (22 x 33 cm) baking dish. Bake, covered, in 425°F (220°C) oven, turning at halftime, for about 1 hour until potato is tender.

Garnish with sour cream and basil sprig. Serves 8.

1 serving: 107 Calories; 3.1 g Total Fat (1.9 g Mono, 0.4 g Poly, 0.6 g Sat); 0 mg Cholesterol; 18 g Carbohydrate; 2 g Fibre; 2 g Protein; 211 mg Sodium

harvest medley

A slow sauté of onions brings out their natural sweetness and caramelizes them. Not only are they a terrific topper for this harvest dish, but they're also wonderful added to mashed potatoes, pizzas and quesadillas. A tiny splash of sherry or port will intensify the onion's sweetness.

Yellow turnip (or rutabaga), diced	1 1/2 lbs.	680 g
Salt	1 tsp.	5 mL
Medium peeled red potatoes, diced	8	8
Butter (not margarine)	1/4 cup	60 mL
Medium onions, thinly sliced	3	3

Pepper, sprinkle

Pour water into large pot or Dutch oven until about 1 inch (2.5 cm) deep. Add turnip and salt. Cover. Bring to a boil. Reduce heat to medium. Boil gently for 5 minutes. Increase heat to medium-high.

Add potato. Cover. Bring to a boil. Reduce heat to medium. Boil gently for 12 to 15 minutes until potato and turnip are tender. Drain. Return to same pot. Reduce heat to low. Cook for 2 minutes, stirring gently, until liquid is evaporated. Transfer to serving bowl. Cover to keep warm.

Heat butter in large frying pan on medium. Add onion. Cook for about 15 minutes, stirring often, until onion is golden and caramelized. Spoon over potato mixture.

Sprinkle with pepper. Makes about 8 cups (2 L). Serves 8.

1 serving: 200 Calories; 6.4 g Total Fat (1.8 g Mono, 0.3 g Poly, 3.9 g Sat); 17 mg Cholesterol; 34 g Carbohydrate; 3 g Fibre; 3 g Protein; 77 mg Sodium

two-toned scalloped potatoes

For a fabulous presentation that shows off the layers of white and sweet potato, let the ramekins sit for 10 minutes once they're out of the oven. Then run a knife around the inside edge of the ramekins and upend them onto serving plates. Add a few basil leaves for garnish, if you like.

Medium unpeeled red potatoes, thinly sliced	2	2
Fresh medium peeled sweet potato, thinly sliced	1	1
Brie cheese round, thinly sliced	4 oz.	125 g
Whipping cream	2/3 cup	150 mL
Salt	1/2 tsp.	2 mL
Pepper	1/2 tsp.	2 mL
Ground nutmeg	1/4 tsp.	1 mL

Divide first 3 ingredients into 8 equal portions each. To assemble, layer ingredients in 4 greased 1 cup (250 mL) ramekins as follows:

1. Portion of potato
2. Portion of sweet potato
3. Portion of cheese
4. Portion of potato
5. Portion of sweet potato
6. Portion of cheese

Combine remaining 4 ingredients in liquid measure. Pour cream mixture into ramekins. Place on baking sheet with sides. Bake in 350°F (175°C) oven for about 50 minutes until tender. Serves 4.

1 serving: 381 Calories; 22.4 g Total Fat (6.5 g Mono, 0.8 g Poly, 14.0 g Sat); 80 mg Cholesterol; 36 g Carbohydrate; 4 g Fibre; 11 g Protein; 521 mg Sodium

festive scalloped potatoes

Any celebration is made more festive with this tasty casserole. Choose a waxy red- or white-skinned potato for well-defined slices.

Butter (or hard margarine)	1/2 cup	125 mL
All-purpose flour	1/2 cup	125 mL
Paprika	1/2 tsp.	2 mL
Salt	2 tsp.	10 mL
Pepper	1/2 tsp.	2 mL
Milk	4 1/2 cups	1.1 L
Medium peeled potatoes, thinly sliced	8	8
Medium red (or white) onion, thinly sliced, rings separated	1	1

Paprika, sprinkle

Heat butter in small saucepan on medium. Add next 4 ingredients. Heat and stir for 1 minute.

Slowly add milk, stirring constantly with whisk. Heat and stir until boiling and thickened.

To assemble, layer ingredients in greased 3 quart (3 L) casserole as follows:

1. Half of potato slices
2. Half of onion slices
3. Half of milk mixture
4. Remaining potato slices
5. Remaining onion slices
6. Remaining milk mixture

Sprinkle second amount of paprika over top. Bake, covered, in 350°F (175°C) oven for 1 hour. Bake, uncovered, for about 10 minutes until golden and potato is tender. Serves 8.

1 serving: 294 Calories; 12.8 g Total Fat (3.5 g Mono, 0.4 g Poly, 8.0 g Sat); 39 mg Cholesterol; 40 g Carbohydrate; 3 g Fibre; 10 g Protein; 739 mg Sodium

italian potato casserole

Evaporated milk gives this dish a wonderful creaminess without the calories. The Roma tomatoes and Parmesan cheese add to its flavour. Magnifico!

Olive (or cooking) oil	1 tsp.	5 mL
Medium onion, sliced	1	1
Garlic clove, minced (or 1/4 tsp., 1 mL, powder)	1	1
Skim evaporated milk	1 cup	250 mL
All-purpose flour	3 tbsp.	50 mL
Prepared mustard	2 tsp.	10 mL
Dried basil	1/2 tsp.	2 mL
Salt	1/2 tsp.	2 mL
Granulated sugar	1/4 tsp.	1 mL
Dried oregano	1/8 tsp.	0.5 mL
Medium unpeeled new potatoes, thinly sliced	4	4
Pepper	1/8 tsp.	0.5 mL
Medium Roma (plum) tomatoes, sliced 1/4 inch (6 mm) thick	4	4
Grated light Parmesan cheese	1 tbsp.	15 mL

Heat olive oil in medium frying pan on medium. Add onion and garlic.

Cook for about 5 minutes, stirring often, until onion is softened.

Stir evaporated milk into flour in small bowl until smooth. Slowly add to onion, stirring constantly, until boiling and thickened. Stir in next 5 ingredients.

To assemble, layer ingredients in greased 2 quart (2 L) casserole as follows:

1. Half of potato slices
2. Half of pepper
3. Half of tomato slices
4. Half of onion mixture
5. Remaining potato slices
6. Remaining pepper
7. Remaining tomato slices
8. Remaining onion mixture

Sprinkle with cheese. Bake, covered, in 375°F (190°C) oven for 45 minutes. Remove cover. Bake for 20 to 30 minutes until top is golden brown and potato is tender. Makes about 5 cups (1.25 L).

3/4 cup (175 mL): 161 Calories; 1.6 g Total Fat (0.8 g Mono, 0.3 g Poly, 0.3 g Sat); 2 mg Cholesterol; 31 g Carbohydrate; 3 g Fibre; 8 g Protein; 337 mg Sodium

potato cakes

Here's a side dish that will quickly take centre stage at any meal. Serve with a hamburger patty or a fried egg and steamed veggies for a fast supper.

Large egg	1	1
Large peeled baking potatoes, grated	3	3
Finely chopped onion	1/2 cup	125 mL
Fine dry bread crumbs	1/4 cup	60 mL
Green onions, chopped	2	2
Seasoned salt	1 tsp.	5 mL
Pepper	1/2 tsp.	2 mL
Cooking oil	2 tbsp.	30 mL

Chopped green onion, for garnish

Combine first 7 ingredients in large bowl.

Divide into 8 equal portions. Shape into 1/2 inch (12 mm) thick cakes. Heat 1 tbsp (15 mL) cooking oil in frying pan on medium. Add 4 cakes. Cook for 12 minutes. Turn. Cook for about 5 minutes until golden. Remove to paper towels to drain. Repeat with remaining cooking oil and cakes.

Garnish with green onion. Makes 8 cakes.

1 cake: 156 Calories; 4.3 g Total Fat (2.4 g Mono, 1.2 g Poly, 0.5 g Sat); 23 mg Cholesterol; 27 g Carbohydrate; 2 g Fibre; 3 g Protein; 219 mg Sodium

potato squares

Square potatoes? It's easy when you grate them and bake them for this easy side. If you don't need to watch your sodium intake, any garlicky seasoning will do.

Large eggs, fork-beaten	2	2
Finely chopped onion	1/2 cup	125 mL
Garlic and herb no-salt seasoning	1/2 tsp.	2 mL
Pepper	1/4 tsp.	1 mL
Peeled potatoes, grated	2 lbs.	900 g
Hot milk	1 cup	250 mL

Combine first 4 ingredients in large bowl. Squeeze potato dry. Add to egg mixture. Stir well.

Slowly add hot milk, stirring constantly until potato is coated. Spread evenly in greased 9 x 9 inch (22 x 22 cm) pan. Bake, uncovered, in 375ºF (190ºC) oven for about 1 hour until golden. Let stand for 5 minutes before cutting. Cuts into 9 pieces.

1 piece: 82 Calories; 1.5 g Total Fat (0.5 g Mono, 0.2 g Poly, 0.6 g Sat); 49 mg Cholesterol; 14 g Carbohydrate; 1 g Fibre; 4 g Protein; 32 mg Sodium

basic smashed and mashed

If you prepare this ahead of time, cover the dish with foil and reheat in a 350°F oven for 30 to 40 minutes. Any leftovers can be used to make Mushroom Cheese Braids, page 58.

Medium peeled potatoes, quartered	10	10
Milk	1/2 cup	125 mL
Sour cream	1/2 cup	125 mL
Hard margarine (or butter)	1/4 cup	60 mL
Onion salt	2 tsp.	10 mL
Salt	1/2 tsp.	2 mL
Pepper	1/8 tsp.	0.5 mL

Grated Parmesan cheese, sprinkle

Green onion pieces, for garnish

Pour water into large pot or Dutch oven until about 1 inch (2.5 cm) deep. Add potato. Cover. Bring to a boil. Reduce heat to medium. Boil gently for 12 to 15 minutes until tender. Drain. Mash.

Add next 6 ingredients. Mash.

Sprinkle with cheese.

Garnish with green onion. Serves 8.

1 serving: 234 Calories; 8.6 g Total Fat (4.7g Mono, 0.8 g Poly, 2.7 g Sat); 7 mg Cholesterol; 36 g Carbohydrate; 3 g Fibre; 4 g Protein; 602 mg Sodium

fluffy garlic potatoes

Baking potatoes have a drier, fluffier texture, which is why we chose them for this dish. Bump up the garlic if you love its flavour.

Medium peeled baking potatoes, quartered	4	4
Salt	1/4 tsp.	1 mL
Low-fat plain yogurt	3 tbsp.	50 mL
Chopped fresh parsley (or 1 1/2 tsp., 7 mL, flakes)	2 tbsp.	30 mL
Garlic clove, minced (or 1/4 tsp., 1 mL, powder)	1	1
Pepper	1/4 tsp.	1 mL

Pour water into large saucepan until about 1 inch (2.5 cm) deep. Add potato and salt. Cover. Bring to a boil. Reduce heat to medium. Boil gently for 12 to 15 minutes until tender. Drain. Mash.

Add remaining 4 ingredients. Beat until smooth and fluffy. Makes about 2 1/2 cups (625 mL).

1/2 cup (125 mL): 115 Calories; 0.3 g Total Fat (0.1 g Mono, 0.1 g Poly, 0.1 g Sat); 1 mg Cholesterol; 25 g Carbohydrate; 2 g Fibre; 3 g Protein; 16 mg Sodium

creamy parsnip mashed potatoes

You can make this up to two hours ahead, letting it stand at room temperature in a covered casserole. To reheat, bake, covered, in a 375°F (190°C) oven for about 30 minutes or until heated through.

Cut up peeled baking potato	8 cups	2 L
Parsnips, chopped	2 lbs.	900 g
Block of light cream cheese, softened	8 oz.	250 g
Sour cream	1 cup	250 mL
Grated Parmesan cheese	1/2 cup	125 mL
Chopped fresh chives	1/3 cup	75 mL
Butter (or hard margarine)	2 tbsp.	30 mL
Pepper	1/2 tsp.	2 mL

Chopped fresh chives, for garnish

Pour water into large pot or Dutch oven until about 1 inch (2.5 cm) deep. Add potato and parsnip. Cover. Bring to a boil. Reduce heat to medium. Boil gently for 12 to 15 minutes until tender. Drain. Mash.

Add next 6 ingredients. Mash.

Garnish with chives. Serves 12.

1 serving: 253 Calories; 10.5 g Total Fat (3.1 g Mono, 0.4 g Poly, 6.2 g Sat); 30 mg Cholesterol; 34 g Carbohydrate; 4 g Fibre; 8 g Protein; 269 mg Sodium

heaven and earth

The name of this old German recipe refers to the fact that the apples must be plucked from above, from the heavens, while the potatoes are dug out of the earth. The combination is truly heavenly.

Peeled potatoes, chopped	2 lbs.	900 g
Salt	1 tsp.	5 mL
Sliced peeled cooking apple, (such as McIntosh) see Tip, page 64	1 1/2 cups	375 mL
Bacon slices, diced	8	8
Medium onion, chopped	1	1
Apple slices, for garnish		

Pour water into large pot or Dutch oven until about 1 inch (2.5 cm) deep. Add potato and salt. Cover. Bring to a boil. Reduce heat to medium. Boil gently for 7 to 8 minutes until tender-crisp. Add apple. Bring to a boil. Reduce heat to medium. Boil gently for 4 to 5 minutes until tender. Drain. Return to same pot. Cover to keep warm.

Cook bacon in medium frying pan on medium for about 4 minutes until starting to brown.

Add onion. Cook, stirring often, until bacon is brown and onion is softened. Drain well. Coarsely mash potato and apple. Stir in 3/4 of onion mixture. Transfer to serving bowl. Sprinkle with remaining onion mixture.

Garnish with apple slices. Makes about 5 cups (1.25 L).

1 cup (250 mL): 194 Calories; 4.6 g Total Fat (2.0 g Mono, 0.6 g Poly, 1.6 g Sat); 7 mg Cholesterol; 36 g Carbohydrate; 4 g Fibre; 4 g Protein; 140 mg Sodium

gnocchi

NYOH-kee is Italian for "dumplings." Use baking potatoes, because they contain less moisture than thin-skinned potatoes. Toss these with your favourite pesto, or cover with tomato sauce and a liberal sprinkling of Parmesan.

Unpeeled baking potatoes	2 lbs.	900 g
Large egg, fork-beaten	1	1
All-purpose flour	2 1/4 cups	550 mL
Melted margarine (or butter)	2 tsp.	10 mL
Salt	1 tsp.	5 mL
Water	16 cups	4 L
Salt	2 tsp.	10 mL

Pour water into large pot or Dutch oven until about 1 inch (2.5 cm) deep. Add potatoes. Cover. Bring to a boil. Reduce heat to medium. Boil gently for 10 to 12 minutes until tender. Drain. Let stand until cool enough to handle. Peel. Mash. Make well in centre.

Add next 4 ingredients. Mix until soft dough forms. Divide dough into 6 portions. Roll 1 portion of dough into 1/2 inch (12 mm) rope. Cut into 1 inch (2.5 cm) pieces. Press fork tines into side of each piece. Repeat with remaining dough portions.

Combine water and salt in large pot. Bring to a boil. Add half of gnocchi. Boil, uncovered, for 2 to 4 minutes until gnocchi float to the top. Transfer with slotted spoon to serving bowl. Repeat with remaining gnocchi. Makes about 96 gnocchi.

12 gnocchi: 181 Calories; 1.6 g Total Fat (0.7 g Mono, 0.3 g Poly, 0.4 g Sat); 22 mg Cholesterol; 37 g Carbohydrate; 2 g Fibre; 5 g Protein; 290 mg Sodium

parker house pockets

Pair these cheese-filled rolls with soup or a summer salad for a filling meal.

Light ricotta cheese	1 cup	250 mL
Green onions, finely sliced	4	4
Skim milk	1 1/4 cups	300 mL
Small peeled potato, cooked and mashed	1	1
Granulated sugar	1/3 cup	75 mL
Canola oil	1/4 cup	60 mL
Salt	3/4 tsp.	4 mL
Whole-wheat flour	2 cups	500 mL
Envelope of instant yeast (or 2 1/4 tsp., 11 mL)	1/4 oz.	8 g
Egg white (large)	1	1
All-purpose flour	2 cups	500 mL
All-purpose flour, approximately	1/2 cup	125 mL

Combine cheese and green onion in small bowl. Set aside.

Combine next 5 ingredients in small saucepan. Heat and stir on medium until sugar is dissolved. Cool until warm.

Combine whole-wheat flour and yeast in extra-large bowl. Stir in potato mixture until thick batter consistency. Add egg white. Mix well.

Add first amount of all-purpose flour, 1/2 cup (125 mL) at a time, until soft dough forms. Turn out onto lightly floured surface. Knead for 5 to 10 minutes, adding second amount of all-purpose flour 1 tbsp. (15 mL) at a time if necessary to prevent sticking, until smooth and elastic. Place in greased extra-large bowl, turning once to grease top. Cover with greased wax paper and tea towel. Let stand in oven with light on and door closed for about 15 minutes until doubled in bulk. Punch dough down. Cut dough in half. Roll one portion out on lightly floured surface to 1/2 inch (12 mm) thickness. Cut with 3 inch (7 cm) round cutter. Place 1 tsp. (5 mL) cheese mixture in middle of round. Fold dough over filling. Pinch edges firmly together to seal. Repeat with remaining dough and filling. Arrange on 2 large greased baking sheets. Cover with greased wax paper and tea towel. Let stand in oven with light on and door closed for about 40 minutes until doubled in size. Bake, uncovered, on separate racks, in 350°F (175°C) oven for 20 to 25 minutes, switching position of baking sheets at halftime, until golden brown. Makes 24 pockets.

1 pocket: 144 Calories; 3.6 g Total Fat (1.7 g Mono, 0.9 g Poly, 0.8 g Sat); 3.5 mg Cholesterol; 24 g Carbohydrate; 2 g Fibre; 5 g Protein; 108 mg Sodium

mushroom cheese braids

Fold one "arm" over another to braid this easy side that doubles as a starter. If you're not into fiddling, just fold uncut edges over the filling.

CRUST

Large egg	1	1
Mashed potato (about 1 lb., 454 g, uncooked)	2 cups	500 mL
All-purpose flour	1 1/4 cups	300 mL
Grated Parmesan cheese	2 tbsp.	30 mL
Salt	1/2 tsp.	2 mL
Pepper	1/4 tsp.	1 mL

FILLING

Hard margarine (or butter)	1 tbsp.	15 mL
Sliced fresh white mushrooms	1 1/2 cups	375 mL
Grated Gruyère cheese	1 cup	250 mL
Chopped green onion	1/4 cup	60 mL
Parsley flakes	1 tsp.	5 mL
Garlic powder (optional)	1/4 tsp.	1 mL
Large egg, fork-beaten	1	1
Grated Parmesan cheese, sprinkle		

Crust: Combine all 6 ingredients in medium bowl until soft dough forms. Divide into 2 equal portions. Roll each portion on well-floured surface to 12 x 9 inch (30 x 22 cm) rectangle.

Filling: Heat margarine in large frying pan on medium. Add mushrooms. Cook, stirring often, until browned. Remove to medium bowl. Cool slightly.

Add next 4 ingredients. Stir. Spoon half of filling lengthwise along 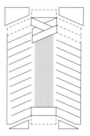 centre of dough rectangle. Cut perpendicular slits in dough about 1 inch (2.5 cm) apart from mushroom mixture outward to edges. Fold strips to cross over mushroom mixture in braid design. Repeat with remaining dough and mushroom mixture.

Carefully transfer to greased baking sheet using pancake lifter. Brush tops with second amount of egg. Sprinkle with Parmesan cheese. Bake in 375°F (190°C) oven for 25 to 30 minutes until golden brown. Cuts into 6 slices per braid.

1 slice: 154 Calories; 5.5 g Total Fat (1.9 g Mono, 0.6 g Poly, 2.4 g Sat); 47 mg Cholesterol; 19 g Carbohydrate; 1 g Fibre; 7 g Protein; 191 mg Sodium

onion and potato tart

Use any left-over pastry for cutouts to decorate the top.

Pastry for 10 inch (25 cm) pie shell	2	2
Medium peeled potatoes, cut up	3	3
Salt	1 tsp.	5 mL
Grated Gruyère cheese	1 1/4 cups	300 mL
Dried thyme	1/2 tsp.	2 mL
Hard margarine (or butter)	1 1/2 tbsp.	25 mL
Coarsely chopped onion	4 1/2 cups	1.1 L
Ground nutmeg	1/8 tsp.	0.5 mL
Seasoned salt	1 tsp.	5 mL
Pepper, generous sprinkle		
Large eggs	5	5
Homogenized milk	1 1/2 cups	375 mL

Roll out pastry on lightly floured surface to about 1/8 inch (3 mm) thickness. Line 10 inch (25 cm) pie plate. Trim, leaving 1/2 inch (12 mm) overhang. Roll under and crimp decorative edge. Cover pastry in pie plate with parchment paper, bringing paper up over edge. Fill halfway up side with dried beans. Place pie plate and cut pastry on ungreased baking sheet. Bake on bottom rack in 375°F (190°C) oven for 15 minutes. Remove pie plate from oven. Bake cut pastry for another 2 to 3 minutes until firm and golden. Carefully remove paper and beans, reserving beans for next time you bake pastry. Let pie shell and pastry pieces stand on wire rack for 10 minutes.

Pour water into large saucepan until about 1 inch (2.5 cm) deep. Add potato and salt. Cover. Bring to a boil. Reduce heat to medium. Boil gently for 12 to 15 minutes until tender. Drain. Let stand until cool. Break potatoes into pea-sized pieces with fork or pastry blender. Spoon into pie shell. Do not pack. Sprinkle with cheese and thyme.

Heat margarine in large frying pan on medium. Add onion. Cook for about 15 minutes, stirring often, until softened. Reduce heat to low. Add next 3 ingredients. Cook, covered, for about 10 minutes, stirring occasionally, until onion is browned and very soft. Spoon over cheese.

Beat eggs and milk together in small bowl using fork. Carefully pour over onion mixture. Bake on bottom rack in 375°F (190°C) oven for 55 to 60 minutes until egg is set and crust is golden. Let stand on wire rack for 10 minutes. Cuts into 8 wedges.

1 wedge: 412 Calories; 23.3 g Total Fat (9.9 g Mono, 2.4 g Poly, 9.2 g Sat); 161 mg Cholesterol; 37 g Carbohydrate; 2 g Fibre; 14 g Protein; 507 mg Sodium

recipe index

topical tips

Fresh apple pieces: To keep apple slices or cubes from turning brown, dip them in lemon juice.

Prepping potatoes: You can ready potatoes ahead of time. Peel them (if necessary), cube, shred or otherwise prepare them and then cover them in water to prevent browning. Don't work too far in advance though, because holding potatoes in water for more than two hours leeches out valuable nutrients.

Storing garlic: Fresh garlic should be stored at room temperature in a cool, dry place. Refrigeration will dehydrate the cloves, affecting their flavour, and may result in other refrigerated foods absorbing their odour.

Storing potatoes: Keep whole, unpeeled potatoes in a cool (not refrigerated), dry place that is well ventilated. Under these conditions they should last several weeks. Stored at room temperature, potatoes should be used within one week. If potatoes begin to green or sprout prior to use, those areas can just be trimmed.

Nutrition Information Guidelines

Each recipe is analyzed using the Canadian Nutrient File from Health Canada, which is based on the United States Department of Agriculture (USDA) Nutrient Database.

- If more than one ingredient is listed (such as "butter or hard margarine"), or if a range is given (1 – 2 tsp., 5 – 10 mL), only the first ingredient or first amount is analyzed.

- For meat, poultry and fish, the serving size per person is based on the recommended 4 oz. (113 g) uncooked weight (without bone), which is 2 – 3 oz. (57 – 85 g) cooked weight (without bone) — approximately the size of a deck of playing cards.

- Milk used is 1% M.F. (milk fat), unless otherwise stated.

- Cooking oil used is canola oil, unless otherwise stated.

- Ingredients indicating "sprinkle," "optional" or "for garnish" are not included in the nutrition information.

- The fat in recipes and combination foods can vary greatly depending on the sources and types of fats used in each specific ingredient. For these reasons, the count of saturated, monounsaturated and polyunsaturated fats may not add up to the total fat content.